Lost Attractions
of Florida's
MIRACLE STRIP

Lost Attractions

of Florida's

MIRACLE STRIP

································· TIM HOLLIS

THE
History
PRESS

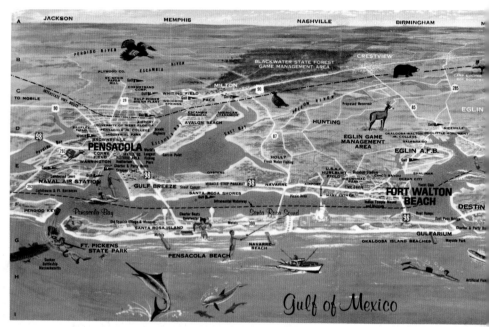

FUN-TRIP FLORIDA'S MIRACLE STRIP
WORLD'S WHITEST BEACHES AND FINEST FISHING

In case anyone needed to know exactly which geographical area made up Florida's famed 130-mile Miracle Strip, this brochure map remained in print for many years. Notice that at this time, I-10 across the Panhandle was merely a dotted line; the map would be periodically updated to reflect the changes in that highway. But even the interstate came nowhere near the main thoroughfare of U.S. 98, which connected Panama City Beach with Destin, Fort Walton Beach and Pensacola. For those who wanted to avoid the prevailing carnival atmosphere in those resorts, there was State Highway 30A and its off-the-beaten-path communities such as Seaside and Watercolor and Grayton Beach – but those are subjects for another book or two that have already been published.

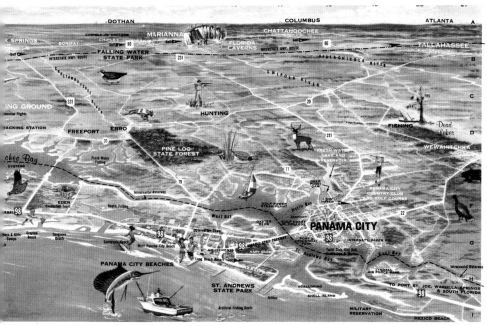

DOTHAN   **COLUMBUS**   **ATLANTA**   A

SPRINGS   BONIFAY   CHIPLEY   **MARIANNA**   CHATTAHOOCHEE   **TALLAHASSEE**

CHIPOLA JR COLLEGE   90   FLORIDA CAVERNS   Gulf   90

Gulf   INTERSTATE HWY. ROUTE   **FALLING WATER STATE PARK**   231   INTERSTATE HWY. ROUTE   APPALACHICOLA RIVER   B

CHOCTAWHATCHEE RIVER   CHIPOLA RIVER

331   20   C

ING GROUND   **HUNTING**

mercial Flights

ACKING STATION   **FREEPORT**   **EBRO**   231   **FISHING**   Dead Lakes

20   **PINE LOG STATE FOREST**   FRESH WATER LAKE AND RESERVOIR   **WEWAHITCHKA**   D

chee Bay   Fresh Water Fishing

OYSTERS   77   DEEP POINT DAM   **PANAMA CITY COUNTRY CLUB**   2880 GOLF COURSE   E

79   Intracoastal Waterway   LYNN HAVEN

KWAY 98   **EDEN** Conducted Tours   Boats, Fishing   **WEST BAY**   NORTH BAY   GULF POWER STEAM PLANT   AIRPORT   22   F

ys & Girls Camps   Crayton Beach   Seagrove Beach   98   Sunnyside Beach   West Panama City Beach   Observation Tower   OYSTER BAR   GULF COAST COLLEGE   **PANAMA CITY**   INTERNAT'L PAPER CO.   GULF BAY

h   AMUSEMENT   98   MIRACLE STRIP PARKWAY   NAVY BASE   PORT INDUSTRIAL PARK   Yacht Club, City Hall, Auditorium & More   Intracoastal Waterway   G

Long Beach Resort—Cottages   St. Andrews Bay

PANAMA CITY BEACHES   **ST. ANDREWS STATE PARK**   TYNDALL AIR FORCE BASE   H

SCALLOPING   TO PORT ST. JOE, WAKULLA SPRINGS & SOUTH FLORIDA

Artificial Fishing Reefs   SHELL ISLAND   Jetties   98

MILITARY RESERVATION   MEXICO BEACH   I

---

s Miracle Strip is a 100-mile-long family resort area ng along the top of the Gulf of Mexico from Pensacola ma City. The Miracle Strip is named for its miraculously ıl bathing beaches . . . a wide shoreline of soft, sugar-

white sand gently sloping into the surf. Here and in adjacent bays and bayous water sports are popular March to November and fishing is excellent almost year round. The Miracle Strip offers more than 40,000 motel rooms and a variety of other facilities.

Thrift-season rates usually apply Labor Day to May 15, which means that in this period you can enjoy comfortable accommodations for as little as six or seven dollars a night. Low weekly and monthly rates also available at many places in Fall and Winter.

Published by The History Press
Charleston, SC
www.historypress.com

Front cover, bottom: Cariss Dooley collection.
Back cover, top: John Margolies collection; *bottom*: Kenneth Redd collection.

Unless otherwise noted, all images are courtesy of the author.

First published 2022

Manufactured in the United States

ISBN 9781467150330

Library of Congress Control Number: 2021949172

CONTENTS

ACKNOWLEDGEMENTS

Although most of the material you will see in the pages that follow originated in my own decades-long collection of memorabilia, credit must be given to the additional sources that enlivened the result. As you will notice in the credit lines for the photos, a number of them (as well as other helpful information) came from fellow tourism collectors and photographers: Becky Craddock, Cariss Dooley, the late Neal Frisbie, Jeri Good, Bill Hudson, Jeremy Kennedy, the late Melody May, Scott Mims, Carey Rayburn, Mat Raymond, Kenneth Redd, Brian Rucker, Adam Sandy, Debra Jane Seltzer, Jack Thomas Jr. and the late Val Valentine.

We must also acknowledge the late photographer John Margolies, who bequeathed his personal archive to the Library of Congress with the amazing stipulation that no restrictions were to be imposed on its use by other authors and researchers.

INTRODUCTION

Welcome, friends, to the latest volume in the ongoing "Lost Attractions" series. For those who are new in this neighborhood, perhaps it would be best to begin by explaining the title. Just what is a "lost attraction" of Florida's Miracle Strip, anyway? Well, it is very simple. A lost attraction can be any type of tourism-related business—roadside attraction, motel, restaurant or other—that no longer exists. Casually flipping through the pages, one may conceivably run across an image and comment, "Hey, that place is still there!" That brings us to the secondary definition: a business that has changed radically over the years and no longer resembles its depiction in vintage photos and postcards, even though, technically, it may still be operating. Everything clear now?

Since the name *Miracle Strip* is not used nearly as often today as it was even twenty-five years ago, perhaps a definition of that term is in order here as well. It originally referred to the beaches of Okaloosa Island when newspaper writer Claude Jenkins coined it in 1952. Within a few years, tourism promoters had begun applying it to the approximately 130 miles of the Florida Panhandle from Panama City on the eastern end to Pensacola on the western end. Altogether, the Miracle Strip was an advertising creation— and some might say a state of mind—rather than a true geographical entity.

Because its commercial development came along so much later than most of the rest of the state, for a long time, the resorts and attractions of the Panhandle were barely considered a part of Florida at all. Panama City Beach was mostly inaccessible until the late 1930s, and the other future resorts did not see their biggest years until after World War II. Pensacola had plenty of U.S. history in its DNA, but heading east from there, it was the state capital at Tallahassee that was the next important point.

Another factor made the Miracle Strip different from anywhere else in Florida. From the time wealthy tourists from the North began riding the rails into Florida in the late 1800s, the state's subtropical climate had made it a winter resort. By the 1930s, that was still its big selling point, although major attractions including Silver Springs and Cypress Gardens, in central Florida, were becoming more popular as year-round destinations. Such was not the case in the Panhandle, where the climate was certainly more subtropical than, say, Nashville, but that did not enjoy the year-round summertime of Miami.

Therefore, until more recent years, the Miracle Strip resorts were tied to a strict operating schedule. They opened on Memorial Day and closed on Labor Day. Eventually, the tradition of spring break pushed the opening back by a month or two, but after Labor Day, one would find the beach a most desolate place. Attractions, motels and restaurants would be shuttered until time to reopen in the spring, so it was desperately necessary for the owners to make their living wage for the year in only a few short months.

The character of the Miracle Strip had changed so much by the 1990s—condos had replaced small two-story motels and the operating season had grown to twelve months from three—that the old name smacked of a bygone era. Practically everywhere it was used, the Miracle Strip became the Emerald Coast, and that truly seemed to signal that the days of the attractions covered in the following pages were really and truly part of the past.

Folks, you are looking at a most historic image. This was the first day your beloved author ever played miniature golf, and it took place at Panama City Beach's colorful Zoo-Land Golf course. Apparently, an octopus was one of the most popular obstacles in Miracle Strip mini-golf, because we are going to be seeing multiple variations of it once we get to Chapter Three.

CHAPTER ONE

COASTERS AND COTTON CANDY

The beach and amusement parks have gone hand in sandy hand for nearly as long as the idea of a man-made playground has existed. In North America, of course, it was the emergence of New York's Coney Island in the late 1800s and early 1900s that truly cemented the relationship between the two. It may seem a bit surprising, then, that the tourist spots of the Miracle Strip took so relatively long to buy into the idea.

Part of that is due to the region itself being a "late bloomer," as it were, in the world of Florida tourism. By the early 1940s, a few temporary amusement rides had been set up at Long Beach Resort for the short duration of the tourist season, but anyone passing by that spot from late September through mid-May would have seen only an empty lot.

It was 1963 before a permanent amusement park lifted its head over the snow-white sands, and, irony of ironies, its early existence was due to some tragic events several hundred miles away. In the spring of that year, the city of Birmingham, Alabama, responded to the protests calling for desegregating the city's facilities by simply closing all city-owned parks. These included Kiddieland, a seasonal amusement center located at the state fairgrounds. Like Long Beach Resort, most of Kiddieland's rides were not permanent structures. So, once word came that they were not going to be needed in Birmingham, the rides were trucked down to Panama City Beach and joined the new Starliner roller coaster to become the nucleus of Miracle Strip Amusement Park.

The immediate success of MSAP, as it was often abbreviated, soon spawned other parks. We will visit at least one of them later in this chapter and a more direct imitator in Chapter Two. For now, remember to keep your hands and arms inside the ride vehicle, and let's go!

OPPOSITE, TOP: As this 1941 postcard shows, even by that early point in Miracle Strip history, temporary rides were being erected at Long Beach Resort for the duration of the tourist season. Note the unlicensed, but amusing, cartoon characters on the kiddie car ride in the foreground.

OPPOSITE, BOTTOM: By the time of this 1966 Long Beach Resort view, the summertime amusement rides had grown in size and scope, if not in permanency. Things were already happening at the western end of the beach that would soon put a stop to this original Long Beach Resort amusement park.

ABOVE: As noted a few pages earlier, it was in 1963 that the Miracle Strip Amusement Park (MSAP) made its debut with some borrowed rides from Birmingham and the spectacular Starliner roller coaster. Park owner Jimmy Lark had enlisted the help of one of the most renowned coaster designers in the industry, James Allen, to come up with the centerpiece for his new park. This is how it looked during that initial season. *Kenneth Redd collection.*

The first MSAP rides were little different than the ones seen at scores of traveling carnivals across the country. In the distance, we can see the smoking crater of the Jungle Land volcano—but that story will have to wait until Chapter Four. *Kenneth Redd collection.*

OPPOSITE, TOP: Another early feature of MSAP was the Haunted Castle dark ride, designed by another leader in his field, Bill Tracy. This elaborate animated façade was meant to evoke the ride's other moniker, Hour Thirteen. *Kenneth Redd collection.*

OPPOSITE, BOTTOM: Even with all the other park attractions, both permanent and temporary, the Starliner coaster remained the centerpiece. Thus, it received some of the most eye-catching signage.

TOP: This aerial view of MSAP was taken in June 1971. The park was still looking a bit sparse compared to how it would appear during the next thirty years. In the upper left corner, the large area of barren dirt was the construction site for MSAP's log flume ride, a concept that had originated with larger parks such as Six Flags.

BOTTOM: This postcard view was taken from approximately the same angle as the 1971 photo, but a couple of years later. The log flume had been finished, and many other rides had filled in the gaps among the permanent buildings.

In 1966, Jimmy Lark called on artist and designer Val Valentine to come up with a walk-through haunted house attraction (as opposed to the Haunted Castle dark ride). Valentine's answer was the Old House. It did not rely on mechanical effects or people in makeup jumping out to scare visitors; instead, the visitors frightened themselves by interacting with the Old House's structural elements, such as a balcony that threatened to collapse under their weight. *Cariss Dooley collection.*

Once Val Valentine began designing for MSAP, he got his fingers into all sorts of materials, including this fudge stand. His "Valentine's Since 1891" sign must have been an inside joke of some sort. The rocking chair on the roof eerily rocked back and forth under its own power—thus proving things at MSAP could get a little creepy even when they weren't meant to be.

OPPOSITE, TOP: Around 1976, Val Valentine's workload at MSAP increased considerably. One of his assignments was to revamp the exterior of the Haunted Castle, dumping Bill Tracy's Hour Thirteen paraphernalia in favor of a leering tree for an entrance and fashioning other sinister architecture. The interior remained basically unchanged.

OPPOSITE, MIDDLE: Valentine was also tasked with sprucing up some of the park's traditional rides by placing them inside new themed buildings. Dante's Inferno was a spinning, tilting Trabant ride housed inside a grinning devil's head. That's Val himself posing with Alan Lark as the new Old Nick nears completion.

OPPOSITE, BOTTOM: Another Valentine building was the Abominable Sno'Man, covering a Scrambler ride in an icy landscape. Valentine's background as a cartoonist with the famed Max Fleischer animation studio can be seen in the yeti's Popeye-shaped forearms.

The Starliner coaster hardly needed anything to make it livelier and more exciting, but Val Valentine thought this gaping dragon's mouth might slay the riders. Maybe this was the cousin of the departed Haunted Castle dragon.

Valentine created this stunning artwork for an ad that was used over and over again in the late 1960s. MSAP, Jungle Land and the Top O' the Strip scenic tower enjoyed only a cursory relationship, but since all three were adjacent to one another, they were frequently grouped together for publicity purposes.

By the early 1980s, customized rides were less common, but the existing rides became flashier and glitzier, as these two 1981 shots amply illustrate. *Both, Cariss Dooley collection.*

Here's that familiar angle showing the entire park again, and as a bonus, we can also see the overflowing parking lot on a summer night in 1980. One publicity writer stated that, at times, it seemed MSAP's lights were so bright that they could be seen all the way from the Alabama/Florida state line. While that might not have been strictly true, these photos show that it wasn't a total exaggeration. *Both, Cariss Dooley collection.*

This commemorative plastic cup was issued as part of MSAP's twentieth anniversary celebration in 1983. The park would survive to observe its thirtieth and fortieth, as well—but then things got sad, as we shall soon see.

OPPOSITE, TOP: The other Miracle Strip resorts knew better than to try anything resembling MSAP. Pensacola Beach stayed out of the amusement park game completely, but Fort Walton Beach did dip its toes into the water with its Okaloosa Island Park (renamed Funway Park in the late 1970s). In this postcard view of the back of the Gulfarium, the entire Okaloosa Island Park layout, including the Comet roller coaster, can be glimpsed across the street.

OPPOSITE, MIDDLE: Photos of Okaloosa Island Park/Funway Park are as rare as snowmen on the beach, for some reason. This image of the park's petting zoo, which was built around a Fairyland theme, is one of the few. And it exists only because it was once used in a Fort Walton Beach publicity brochure.

OPPOSITE, BOTTOM: After Okaloosa/Funway Park gasped its last, the skeletal remains of its Comet roller coaster still sat forlornly in the overgrown lot. Amusement park historian Adam Sandy took this photo of the Comet and its red-white-blue paint scheme in 1995, shortly before it met its final doom. Today, the property is the site of Fort Walton Beach's civic center complex. *Adam Sandy collection.*

ABOVE: Meanwhile, back at MSAP, there were plans to develop the property for condos, which would be far more profitable than an amusement park that operated for only a few months each year. On Labor Day 2004, the bright lights were shut off for the last time. This depressing photo was taken in May 2006, when the Starliner coaster had been dismantled. It subsequently operated for a while at Cypress Gardens in central Florida, but as of this writing it currently sits in storage, awaiting its next adventure.

TOP: More than five years after its closing, the MSAP entrance sign still stood bravely over its former domain.

BOTTOM: Believe it or not, here we are back with our familiar angle—only it doesn't look so familiar anymore. Ever since the planned condo project fell through, the MSAP property has been allowed to sit unused, becoming more and more overgrown with foliage. A person who had never seen the park would hardly suspect that anything of its type ever existed on this spot.

CHAPTER TWO

DUEL IN THE DUNES

Another type of amusement park existed that was so different from the specimens dissected in Chapter One that it deserves a closer look of its own. There was nothing particularly unique about the idea of a park based on a Wild West theme. In fact, in those late 1950s–early 1960s days, when every other television program seemed to be a variation on a cowboy and his horse, Western parks proliferated throughout the country. Some, such as Knott's Berry Farm in California and Frontier City in Oklahoma City, looked reasonably authentic in their settings, but plenty of others seemed incongruously out of place.

That brings us back to Panama City Beach and its battle of those two ornery owlhoots, Tombstone Territory and Petticoat Junction. The reasons for trying to recreate the Old West on the Gulf Coast might be too much to try to figure out in our limited space, but what is certain is that their dual emergence within a year of each other had as much to do with dueling tourism as it did with anyone's love for the Hollywood Western genre. Simply put, the competition between Long Beach Resort and the newer developments at West Panama City Beach was fierce, and any idea that sprouted in one locale was likely to inspire a copy at the other end of the beach before the ink on the blueprints was even dry.

In this chapter, we will see how each of these two Western park podners began slowly and then added more and more features in order to one-up the other. It's time to saddle up and ride off into the subtropical Florida scrub brush, with occasional detours into sights even more bizarre than cowboys and outlaws and Native Americans whooping it up among palm trees and white sand.

It all began inconspicuously around 1961, when Lee Koplin of Goofy Golf fame leased a portion of the adjoining property to a skyride operator. At roughly the same time, another concessionaire installed what was advertised as a "frontier train ride," a miniature locomotive that hauled tourists in a circle and back into the forest. However, once in that wooded area, there was initially nothing to see. *Kenneth Redd collection.*

OPPOSITE: The skyride was a big hit from the start, because it gave young couples some much-desired privacy. And, until the mid-1960s, it was taller than any other structure on the beach. Like the train ride, it traveled in a circle, reaching the end of its cable and then returning riders to their same starting point. *Kenneth Redd collection.*

Other features soon sprouted in the backside of the Koplin property, including the Magic Forest and its collection of animated fairy-tale dioramas. This conglomeration of sights was dubbed "Magic World" by Lee Koplin, and his giant concrete rendition of a genie emerging from Aladdin's lamp was an effective roadside lure. (In this angle, note the Surf Motel in the spot that would later be occupied by Castle Dracula.) *Jack Thomas Jr. collection.*

Lee Koplin decided to build an entire Western town at the halfway point of the train ride. He named it Tombstone Territory (after one of the many TV Westerns of the day). For one season, this huge billboard served to let people know the town was there. The billboard would soon be replaced by something even bigger.

Koplin's masterpiece of concrete was this massive replica of Colorado's Mesa Verde, impossible to ignore. The seeming ruins housed various ventures, including an "Indian Trading Post" gift shop, and young Native American dancers were hired to entertain those waiting for the miniature train. The structures housed more or less authentic recreations of the Cliff Dwellers' living quarters. Pay special attention to those cattle and that totem pole, as you will be encountering them again soon. *Both, Kenneth Redd collection.*

Somehow, it is difficult to imagine the Native Americans of the American Southwest looking much like these models, but who cares? When not looking at the ladies, visitors could glean the background of the Mesa Verde replica from the hand-painted signage.

OPPOSITE: The "town" portion of Tombstone Territory offered all the sights one might expect from a typical Old West community, including the saloon with its dancing girls kicking up their heels on the stage. A general store, a jail, a Spanish mission and other enterprises helped folks pass the time while waiting for the next train out of town.

OPPOSITE, TOP: This frame from a 1970s promotional film shows just how eye-catching the Tombstone Territory sign, and the giant Native American holding it, would have appeared to anyone cruising the busy strip at night. *Bill Hudson collection.*

OPPOSITE, BOTTOM: While all of this was going on next door to Goofy Golf, over at Long Beach Resort, the Churchwell family had also leased space for a Western-style train ride. One big difference was that theirs was a full-size antique locomotive, as opposed to Tombstone Territory's miniature model. Still, the train tracks simply ran in a circle, with nothing to see except the passing scenery.

ABOVE: Since Panama City Beach's other Western park had been named after a TV show, so would be the one at Long Beach Resort. One of the Churchwells happened to be friends with the gravelly voiced old character actor Edgar Buchanan, who was suddenly a big star again through his role as Uncle Joe on the sitcom *Petticoat Junction*. He arranged to allow the Churchwells to use the name for their new park, even though the only thing it had in common with the show was that both featured a train. *Kenneth Redd collection.*

ABOVE: Tombstone Territory had built a "town" at the midpoint of its railroad, so Petticoat Junction had to do the same. This marvelous view shows practically the entire setup. After it was completed, it was technically known as Ghost Town, while Petticoat Junction was the name applied to the property near the highway where passengers boarded the train. *Kenneth Redd collection.*

OPPOSITE: Ghost Town was somewhat misnamed, with all the activity that went on throughout the day. Over and over again, the worst of the outlaws would rob the bank or break out of jail, and it was up to the marshal to restore law and order. As was traditional for Western parks, somewhere during the gun battle he had to shoot a bad guy off the roof of a building, the varmint landing with a thud on the sandy street below. Digger the Undertaker was the comic-relief figure, serving to lighten the mood. *Both, Kenneth Redd collection.*

OPPOSITE, TOP: Not content to imitate Tombstone Territory, Petticoat Junction also aped Miracle Strip Amusement Park by installing its own rides in the roadside section. Whereas MSAP's roller coaster was custom designed, Petticoat's Tornado coaster had previously operated in Oklahoma. On its arrival in Florida, it was reassembled by Ghost Town's crew of gunfighters. They were reportedly one confused posse when it was finished, as they had a pile of unused parts left over. *Kenneth Redd collection.*

OPPOSITE, BOTTOM: Another addition to Petticoat Junction's roadside section was this giant pirate, which had a previous life as a shopping center's Santa Claus. A bit of fiberglass surgery transformed jolly St. Nick into a bucktoothed buccaneer, and after a brief stint housing a wax museum of pirate scenes, it served as the entrance for a paddleboat ride and the famous Sui-Slide water attraction.

ABOVE: In this masterfully staged shot, the photographer managed to capture the train, the Tornado coaster and the back edge of the paddleboat lagoon all at the same time. Although the park had three different antique locomotives, only one would be used at any given time. In synergy with the TV comedy, each train was known as the Cannonball. *Kenneth Redd collection.*

In this view, we can see the entire scope of Petticoat Junction's amusement park and even a small portion of the Ghost Town at the far left edge. It is obvious that Petticoat occupied the property across the street from the original Long Beach attractions, many of which were still operating as well. *Mat Raymond collection.*

OPPOSITE, TOP: One of the amusement park's features was this Magic Carpet dark ride, versions of which could be found at various parks throughout the country. Using the same principle as Disney's Peter Pan ride, the simulated magic carpets were suspended above the floor rather than traveling on a guide bar. The actual scenes were left up to the park owners to design and install.

OPPOSITE, BOTTOM: Things were changing rapidly by the time of this late 1970s shot, taken most likely during spring break, as evidenced by the presence of Bud Man, who would have had more appeal to high school and college students than youngsters. Tombstone Territory was now as dead as its name, its sign replaced by a revival of the Magic World name. *Kenneth Redd collection.*

TOP: This photo dates from August 1979, roughly the same period as the Bud Man shot. It is evident that the former Tombstone Territory property was now mostly abandoned, and the skyride had long since stopped its round trips. The skyride's declining popularity, stripped of its novelty, had only been compounded by Hurricane Eloise in 1975, which scattered its dangling buckets far and wide.

BOTTOM: The only visible remnant of the skyride today is this massive platform that served as its turnaround point. Look closely, and you may still be able to make out a couple of the buckets, rusting their way into oblivion.

OPPOSITE: Sometime around 1980, the enormous Mesa Verde/Cliff Dwellers structure was demolished and several smaller, more temporary buildings erected on the site. Oddly, the longhorn cattle and totem pole we saw earlier were left standing in their original locations as the landscape around them evolved. These photos were made in 1989, but today there are no traces of either of these Tombstone Territory survivors.

Tombstone Territory's Iron Horse locomotive was purchased by a collector in Warrior, Alabama. For decades, it sat in this condition under a shed near the individual's home next to I-65. It was recently sold and moved to Mississippi, where, hopefully, it will undergo a restoration to bring it back to its rightful appearance. *Neal Frisbie collection.*

OPPOSITE: As for the "town" portion of Tombstone Territory, most of it still exists, but in the sad condition you see here. It is technically a part of the Raccoon River Campground, and the ruins can be glimpsed inside a fenced-in area. *Jeremy Kennedy collection.*

OPPOSITE· The Spanish mission has been used primarily as a toolshed since the 1980s, but the old padre remains in front just in case any parishioners show up for Sunday services. Even with all the indignities heaped on it, the mission has retained the elaborate murals that were painted on the interior walls.

ABOVE: This swinging bridge actually dates back to the pre–Tombstone Territory days of the Magic Forest. It is somewhat remarkable that it still exists, but of course, no one is allowed to cross it anymore—as if anyone would even take that chance. *Carey Rayburn collection.*

ABOVE: Things weren't any more cheerful over at Petticoat Junction. The amusement park and Ghost Town closed at the end of the 1984 season, and the rides and contents of the buildings were auctioned off. In 1990, the Tornado roller coaster was demolished, and in 1993, the giant pirate burned down. This photo was made shortly thereafter, when the pirate's charred remains provided a melancholy foreground for the decaying Sui-Slide.

OPPOSITE: In 1995, the former Petticoat Junction property became the location for Panama City Beach's mammoth Walmart store. The paddleboat lagoon, seen here in 2013, is still in existence on an out parcel of the Walmart complex, but the Florida foliage has choked it beyond all recognition.

The three locomotives that together depicted the Petticoat Junction Cannonball were purchased by the same collector as the miniature Iron Horse. They now exist in varying degrees of restoration; this is how one of them appeared shortly before its move from Alabama to Mississippi. *Neal Frisbie collection.*

There was actually a third Western ghost town in the Panhandle—sort of. Beginning in 1964, Bellview Junction existed on the grounds of St. Anne's Church in Pensacola; however, it was open for only one weekend each year, when the church put on a spectacular Western roundup with all the usual gunslingers, saloon girls and other accoutrements. Hurricane Ivan erased it from the Pensacola landscape in 2004.

CHAPTER THREE

GOOFY FOR MINIATURE GOLF

The Miracle Strip, in conjunction with adjacent resort areas, was responsible for what historians of the pastime have labeled the "Gulf Coast style" of miniature golf courses. Most people are unaware that, as a commercial enterprise, miniature golf originated in 1925 atop Lookout Mountain, near Chattanooga, Tennessee. Its developer was Garnet Carter, who would carve out a second role in tourism history when he opened Rock City Gardens in 1932. But his concept of Tom Thumb Golf came first and truly emphasized the "miniature" part of the game's moniker.

Players putted about through tiny landscapes and minuscule obstacles, with statues of gnomes enlivening the grounds. Miniature golf became a national craze during the Great Depression, but like most such fads (think fidget spinners, Pogs and other examples), it wore out its welcome quickly. By the end of the 1930s, the very name *miniature golf* was shorthand for something that was hopelessly outdated and good only for fuddy-duddies.

But miniature golf was not dead, only dormant. In the post–World War II years, when the baby boom created millions of new families craving entertainment, miniature golf was revived not as a fad but as a viable component of amusement parks, resort areas and suburban shopping centers. Out in Guerneville, California, former welder Lee Koplin had the idea to spruce up his brother's miniature golf course with some oversized concrete statues. Business increased so much that Koplin decided to make the game his future.

Building ever-larger courses, which he branded as Goofy Golf, along the Gulf Coast, Koplin finally arrived in the Miracle Strip in 1958–59.

Fortunately, as of this writing, all three original Miracle Strip courses are still operating, but that does not mean they have not seen changes. In this chapter, we will see not only some of their elements that no longer exist but also many imitators that tried to make their own goofy holes-in-one among the beach visitors.

OPPOSITE, TOP: Reportedly, the Goofy Golf on Navy Boulevard in Pensacola (not on the beach) opened in 1958. As mentioned at the beginning of this book, an octopus was a standard obstacle at all Goofy Golf courses, and at many others as well. That is the author in Pensacola in 1973.

OPPOSITE, BOTTOM: In the late 1970s, Pensacola's Goofy Golf was given a makeover, importing numerous figures from one of the chain's imitators, Sir Goony Golf. One of the 1958 survivors was the unmistakably creepy Frogman, seen here in 1979. He has since been removed and replaced, as has the green octopus we just saw.

Fort Walton Beach's Goofy Golf on Eglin Parkway (also not at the beach) opened in August 1959 and remains remarkably well preserved in the form in which it appeared on opening day. One of the few casualties was this gruesome creature representing the title character in a 1959 B-grade horror film, *The Monster of Piedras Blancas*. He terrorized young and old with the decapitated woman's head in his hand but fell victim to rowdy high school seniors in 1984.

OPPOSITE: Lee Koplin was not directly involved in the design or construction of the Goofy Golfs in Pensacola and Fort Walton Beach. Instead, he put all of his effort into what would be his flagship course in Panama City Beach, opened in 1959. This sign became a Miracle Strip landmark, as seen here around 1977, but was eventually wiped out by one of the many hurricanes that blew through from time to time. *John Margolies collection.*

What was that we said about every course having an octopus? The original squid at Panama City Beach was quite different from the one most people remember (and which still exists today). As you can see, this first attempt was not even as tall as the players on the course and had a rather nonthreatening expression. *Becky Craddock collection.*

The larger and more fearsome replacement octopus had a writhing mass of tentacles, one of which held aloft a struggling captive mermaid. Like the original Goofy Golf sign, the mermaid did not survive repeated hurricane encounters. With her torso gone, her tail was initially converted into a fish, but now even that is gone and the octopus clutches no victim at all.

Goofy Golf's castle was the home to a brutish ogre with a nightmarish set of fangs, but the plywood meanie had a relatively short life span. The castle spent years uninhabited, but a re-creation of the ogre now peers over its balustrade once more. *Becky Craddock collection.*

OPPOSITE: Goofy Golf's sea monster was originally the entrance to the ticket office. The terror of the deep went through innumerable paint jobs over the decades; the photo with green highlights dates from 1960, while the one with the Day-Glo fluorescent color scheme comes from seventeen years later. In any case, the monster's mouth now has iron bars to prevent anyone from venturing inside, and his two front fangs are also missing in action. The Tooth Fairy must have left a bundle of dough for those babies. *Top, Becky Craddock collection.*

ABOVE: Naturally, Long Beach Resort had to get into the act, too. These two photos from 1960 document an otherwise unidentified course with an amazing variety of concrete inhabitants, from a deformed dragon to Humpty Dumpty to a giant mermaid with formidable upper-body strength. *Both, Becky Craddock collection.*

OPPOSITE, TOP: As with the case of amusement parks mentioned earlier, Pensacola Beach largely stayed out of the prevailing carnival atmosphere of the rest of the Miracle Strip. However, if you will peer closely at the center of this aerial view that was postmarked in 1965, you might be able to make out the shape of some sort of miniature golf course at the edge of the white sand. Unfortunately, its name and any other details remain a mystery.

OPPOSITE, MIDDLE: On the western end of Panama City Beach's development, retired sign painter L.L. Sowell built Zoo-Land Golf in 1960. Some twenty-two years later, that is Sowell himself visible in the window of the ticket office, surveying his creation.

OPPOSITE, BOTTOM: Unlike Goofy Golf, which remains basically the same as it was in 1959, Zoo-Land Golf was in a constantly changing state of flux. Its obstacles and even its fairways could be moved about into different configurations. The date of this photo is undetermined but is unmistakably from Zoo-Land's earliest years. *Cariss Dooley collection.*

ABOVE: Here are two more views from Zoo-Land Golf's first year of operation, when the figures were in even different locations than the early photo we just saw. The motel visible across the street, the Mara-Vista, was later familiar to a generation of visitors as the Tourway Inn. *Both, Becky Craddock collection.*

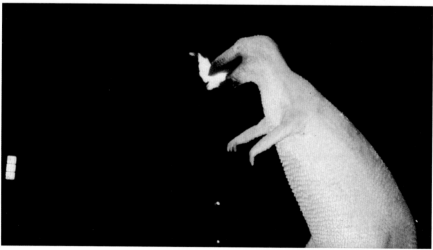

OPPOSITE: L.L. Sowell's pride and joy was his tyrannosaurus, which was not an obstacle but a roadside lure that faced traffic approaching from the west. With a concealed gas pipe inside, the prehistoric monster breathed fire at night—a stunt that no real-life dinosaur has yet been confirmed to have done.

ABOVE: Here is a terrific overview of Zoo-Land Golf from the balcony of the Tourway Inn in 1981. In the mid-1990s, the course was bulldozed and converted into an extension of the property owner's RV park. Even that is now gone, swallowed by the massive bulk of the Emerald Beach Resort.

LEFT: Eventually, L.L. Sowell's brother also decided to go into the miniature golf business, with a small course on Thomas Drive he named Beacon Golf. Appropriately, its roadside lure was a giant simulated lighthouse.

TOP: Beacon Golf's concrete critters were not obstacles but were there strictly for decorative purposes. The property now serves as a motorcycle rental company, with no giant green worm but the former Beacon Golf lighthouse as its only tie to its past.

BOTTOM: In 1972, a new course joined Panama City Beach's lineup. This was Pirate's Cove Golf, and from the very first fairway it was obvious that the seafaring theme was going to be followed to its yo-ho-ho extreme. This sight was guaranteed to frighten children of all ages.

OPPOSITE: During the earliest years of Pirate's Cove Golf, its landscaping was immaculate. The giant Moby Dick in the far corner was as much an attraction for golfers as it had been for Captain Ahab. And, yes, the course would not have been complete without an octopus, just like all the rest.

OPPOSITE, TOP: In case you don't recognize where Pirate's Cove Golf stood, this angle should help you put it in perspective. Next door, past the giant eel and visible over the open treasure chest, is the grandstand for Gulf World, which was also a fairly new attraction when the course opened.

OPPOSITE, BOTTOM: Well, Gulf World is still going strong, but Pirate's Cove Golf went down with the ship only about ten years after it opened. This is how the formerly landscaped lot appears today; it is possible that a few of those palms could be left over from the course, but not very likely.

ABOVE: Because miniature golf courses nationwide had co-opted the Goofy Golf name without authorization, the Koplin family began using the name Magic Carpet Golf for its newer ventures. Since Fort Walton Beach already had a 1959 Goofy Golf, in the late 1970s, the Koplins brought a Magic Carpet Golf to Okaloosa Island.

TOP: As you can see, Magic Carpet Golf greatly resembled Panama City Beach's Goofy Golf, with its eclectic cast of concrete creations. But it had less of the fanciful landscaping and non-obstacle decoration. This wonderful panorama captures almost the entire scope of the property. *John Margolies collection.*

OPPOSITE: The alligator and the monkey grasping a palm tree were two of the Goofy Golf regulars that were re-created in Fort Walton Beach for Magic Carpet Golf. In the monkey photo, which was taken just at sunset, also note the lighted sign for Okaloosa Island's Ramada Inn in the lower left corner.

ABOVE: For whatever reason, half of Magic Carpet Golf was finished by 1979, but the other half took most of the next decade to complete. It hardly seemed worth all that effort, because by the end of the 1990s, it had all been demolished and the property converted into other businesses.

CHAPTER FOUR

TOURISTS' DELIGHTS

After enjoying amusement rides until losing their lunch, watching the marshal shoot outlaws off the roofs of buildings and trying to hit a golf ball into an alligator's mechanical mouth, was there anything else for tourists and their restless offspring to do besides play in the sand and surf? As character actor Frank Nelson might have responded, "Oooooooh, *were* there!!"

The Miracle Strip resort areas were packed with activities, many under common ownership by those who had the foresight to buy up as much highway frontage as possible when it was still relatively cheap (as with Lee Koplin, as we have seen, buying space for Goofy Golf, a skyride and Tombstone Territory, among other ventures). This seemed quite reasonable, considering that most activities did not take very long to complete, leaving visitors eager to move on to something else.

As was mentioned early on in this book, Long Beach Resort was the original amusement hub of the Panama City Beach strip, and its pioneering attractions such as the Hang Out seem to open up an overflowing can of fond memories for those of a certain generation. By ten years later, a new type of attraction had emerged, exemplified by the Jungle Land volcano and the Top O' the Strip observation tower. Still later, the 1970s brought even more attractions to appeal to the disco generation.

Similar goings-on were going on in Fort Walton Beach and Pensacola Beach, although not nearly to the extent as in Panama City Beach. One might think that the long stretch of U.S. 98 that connected them all would have been a constant string of tourist traps, but in fact, there were miles and miles of desolate stretches that could have existed anywhere in the country. But once the bright lights of the next resort appeared on the horizon, there was sure to be something fun in store—and we have it all right here.

The marketing of Panama City Beach really kicked in during the years immediately following World War II. This 1950s brochure spread tried to itemize all the different reasons one might consider the area for fun or business; the blond model's identity is unknown, but she was quite obviously the vanguard for the advertising we will encounter in our final chapter, several pages hence.

As we just said, Long Beach Resort was the center of activity in the 1950s, and the Hang Out was the center of activity at Long Beach Resort. Explaining just why probably depends on one's generation. An open pavilion with a dance floor, where youths from widely varying states and cities could intermingle, had an appeal unique to 1950s teen culture and the desire to get away from parental supervision.

Long Beach's Mystery House is well named, because its existence remains something of a mystery. This is a frame from a 1950s promotional film, and from it we can glean that the Mystery House was somehow written up in *Life* magazine. Knowing the format of similar attractions in other tourist centers, we can probably imagine most of what the shack had to offer. *Bill Hudson collection.*

This is how Long Beach Resort appeared in the early 1960s, with visitors crowding the white sands, the row of red-roofed tourist cottages and amusements of various types spilling from one side of U.S. 98 to the other.

OPPOSITE: Things were much the same by the time of this 1967 magazine ad, with the addition of the Petticoat Junction amusement park and Ghost Town. The rivalry between Long Beach and the growing number of amusements in West Panama City Beach was becoming more vicious, with each having its own set of loyal customers.

Welcome to LONG BEACH RESORT

PANAMA CITY BEACH

FUN FUN FUN

Exciting Pleasure Treasures For The Family. Located on "The World's Most Beautiful Bathing Beaches" with the sugar-white sand stretching for 100 miles along the coast. You will love the blue-green waters with the white-capped surf, and the cool Gulf breeze . . . Making a vacation spot that is never too cool, and never too hot.

Long Beach Resort has the finest restaurants, gifts shops, general stores, just everything that you could need or wish for . . . Whether you stay in a motel, rent a cottage, do your own cooking, or eat in the restaurants, you will find everything at Long Beach Resort.

Everybody loves to relive the Old West at the Petticoat Junction and the Ghost Town Railroad.

The wail of a steam whistle, the smell of smoke, the clackety-clack of the "Ol' Cannonball" pulling up to Petticoat Junction. An abrupt change back to the present when the teen-agers discover the world famous "Hang-Out."

The beautiful Olympic Pool is the largest on Florida's Miracle Strip, and free to everyone staying in the cottages or motels at Long Beach Resort.

LONG BEACH

Bring Your Camera!

DEER RANCH

All ages delight in seeing these gentle animals at the Deer Ranch, which has a collection of over 100 deer; sheep from the Far East; and a real live buffalo . . . named "Bill," of course! The small ones especially love to feed the baby goats, sheep and deer. We have just finished a new "Billy-Goat Hill," so watch the goats climb the Tower, and cross over to "Billy-Goat Hill."

Deer Ranch — Next to the Dolphin Restaurant, Highway 98, Panama City, Florida
Long Beach Resort: Phone Area Code 904 234-2951 or mail to P. O. Box 9283, Panama City, Florida

As an example of the competition that was going on, let's take the Long Beach Deer Ranch. The glorified petting zoo presented dozens of furry friends of all types, vying with kids to see which could look the cutest.

TOP: Over at the skyride/Goofy Golf neighborhood, there was Bambi Land, with its own menagerie of deer, goats and other cuddly critters. This forlorn structure, which was later used as a residence, is the only remnant of Bambi Land, although it is now home to feral cats instead of deer. *Jeremy Kennedy collection.*

BOTTOM: Okay, so not all wildlife was as cute as the residents of Bambi Land and the Long Beach Deer Ranch. From 1946 to 1991, the Snake-A-Torium delighted in presenting exhibits that made visitors' skin crawl. In 1992, it was converted into today's ZooWorld attraction.

It was not imperative for all attractions to have live animals, or even a theme, to draw the crowds. Let's take the case of the red-and-white-striped giant slide visible on the north side of the highway in this view of the Hilton Sun Motel. Slides of its type were a fairly common sight along the Miracle Strip and in other inland amusement zones as well—frequently near those old faithful miniature golf courses.

OPPOSITE: Likely the Ocean Opry show, with its country music theme, appealed to the opposite demographic as the giant slides and the Hang Out. It kept up its hillbilly hoedowns on the strip for decades, and the facility currently serves as a church. *Kenneth Redd collection.*

For years, people wondered what this beachside monstrosity used to be. The answer is rather mundane. It was a bar, curiously named the U-Turn Sunburn Saloon, which was a part of the Rendezvous Motel complex. (This is actually the back of the structure, facing the highway.) It sat in this condition for many years after the Rendezvous was over, but it has now joined the rest of the motel in that great resort in the sky. *Debra Jane Seltzer collection.*

OPPOSITE: A quick view of Pensacola Beach from the air demonstrates its lack of kooky attractions. One of its few diversions was its re-creation of a Spanish settlement, which was not an amusement park but rather looked like just what it was: a group of buildings sitting among the sand dunes. It had been constructed for Pensacola's four-hundredth anniversary in 1959, and afterward was left for tourists to visit until being razed in 1973.

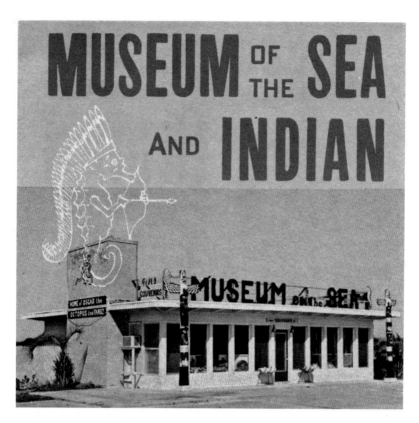

Situated between Destin and Fort Walton Beach, the Museum of the Sea and Indian looked like an attraction from another era, even when it was new. Just its photo op setup, with a Plains Indians tepee alongside a fake alligator and a totem pole, indicated that historical accuracy was not quite as much a concern as it was at, say, Pensacola Beach's Spanish village. The museum became a part of history itself after Hurricane Opal wiped it off the map in 1995.

TOP: One of Panama City Beach's most durable landmarks had its germinal beginning in 1963, when herpetologist Ross Allen of Silver Springs fame opened a branch attraction next door to the new Miracle Strip Amusement Park. He brought his friend, veteran Silver Springs artist Val Valentine, up from Ocala to manage the zoo. *Kenneth Redd collection.*

BOTTOM: In 1965, Valentine purchased the Jungle Show from Ross Allen and operated it for a season as the Seminole Reptile Jungle. Otherwise, its exhibits remained basically the same.

One thing is for sure: with the Seminole Reptile Jungle added to the existing Snake-A-Torium, at no other point in Florida Panhandle history was there such a demand for citizens to go out and capture snaky specimens—and get paid cash for them, too.

OPPOSITE: The Seminole Reptile Jungle showed its Silver Springs origins by hiring genuine Seminole Indians to live on the property and demonstrate their native culture. The animal exhibits also displayed a lot of character, such as this black bear enjoying a Coca-Cola offered by lovely Mary Lynn May. It was not until later that polar bears began drinking Coke.

Realizing that he needed a "package" to attract tourists, Valentine hit upon the idea of housing his exhibits inside a towering volcano with smoke billowing from its crater. To go along with the new theme, the name would be changed to Jungle Land.

OPPOSITE, TOP: The volcano was constructed of wire mesh over a complex of wooden poles, as seen in the previous photo. Here, model Odette Mordelay poses on the swinging bridge while the future volcano is still in its chicken-wire stage.

OPPOSITE, BOTTOM: When completed in the spring of 1966, the Jungle Land volcano looked like nothing else on the Miracle Strip. Its dramatic waterfalls and the billowing smoke made for a sight that few could resist checking out more closely.

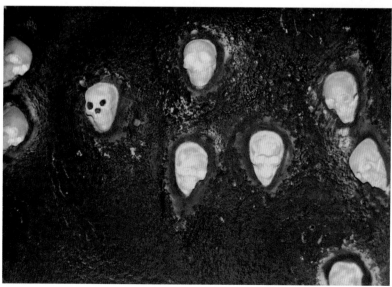

OPPOSITE, TOP: Stationed near the front entrance was a literal barrel of monkeys—the tiny squirrel monkey species, that is. With the prevailing South Pacific theme of Jungle Land, the Seminole exhibits might have seemed a little misplaced, but they were still there regardless.

OPPOSITE, BOTTOM: A walk through the volcano's passageways simulated a "journey to the center of the earth," or at least the center of the volcano. Spooky sights abounded, such as this brace of skulls embedded in one cavern's ceiling. Illuminated by black light and nothing else, they presented a suitably creepy vibe.

ABOVE: With public interest in jungle attractions waning, by 1980–81, Valentine's volcano had become the centerpiece for Alvin's Magic Mountain Mall. This is one of the sealed-up windows from the "center of the earth" walking tour; it formerly looked down on fake molten lava, not displays of beach souvenirs.

After many years of deterioration, by March 2020, it was determined that Alvin's Magic Mountain Mall was no longer structurally sound. It was demolished that spring—the removal of one more landmark of the old Miracle Strip days. *Panama City News-Journal collection.*

OPPOSITE, TOP: Another landmark, opened in April 1966, was the two-hundred-foot-tall Top O' the Strip observation tower. It was a geometric masterpiece and dwarfed any other structures of that day along the beach. A motel was considered a skyscraper if it had four stories, and the old skyride supports looked like matchsticks compared to the tower.

OPPOSITE, BOTTOM: The metal skeleton of the towering tower received more wear and tear from the salt air off the Gulf than usual for a structure of its size, and by the early 1990s, the elevator had stopped running. After Hurricane Opal blew over the coast in 1995, the tower was in no shape to continue its purpose, and it was imploded in December of that year.

OPPOSITE, TOP: While it existed, the tower provided an unparalleled view of the Miracle Strip and all of its attractions. This shot was taken from its observation deck in June 1971. It is not hard to pick out Jungle Land, Goofy Golf and Tombstone Territory, but the skyride's support poles are also visible.

OPPOSITE, BOTTOM: But how about this sight, eh? Some photographer struck gold with this 1968 nighttime view of the strip, also possibly taken from the Top O' the Strip platform. It looks like a capacity crowd at the Miracle Strip Amusement Park and the colorfully lighted volcano; note the continuous stream of headlights on the highway, thanks to the time exposure necessary for a dark image such as this.

ABOVE: In the mid-1970s, a new attraction slunk into the neighborhood. Castle Dracula was promoted as a wax museum, but that was not strictly correct. Its monsters were not wax figures but ordinary mannequins wearing Don Post Halloween masks. *Kenneth Redd collection.*

Castle Dracula's ads were careful to not promise too much. They did score points for the creative slogan, "We'll be lurking for you!"

OPPOSITE: There are no known photos of Castle Dracula's interior, probably because fewer people would have paid the admission price if they knew how it looked. Most tourists were content to take photos with the costumed Frankenstein's monster, who endured the summer heat on the sidewalk in front of the castle. The entire structure burned to the ground in the early 1980s. *Scott Mims collection.*

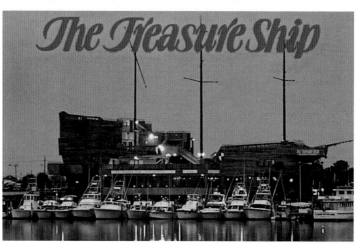

OPPOSITE: Another attraction that eventually fell victim to the flames was the Treasure Ship, a collection of themed restaurants, gift shops, lounges and arcades that sat alongside Thomas Drive. *Kenneth Redd collection.*

ABOVE: Before leaving this chapter, let's take another look at the view from the tower's observation deck, this time in June 1977. Changing times are evident by the almost-empty parking lot at Jungle Land; the turrets of Castle Dracula can be seen just beyond the Tombstone Territory Cliff Dwellers' structure. Within a few years, there would be no recognizable remains of any of it except for Goofy Golf, stubbornly sticking to its patch of sand.

CHAPTER FIVE

SIGNS OF FUN AHEAD

Sometimes it seemed that there were so many attractions crowded onto the Miracle Strip beaches that there was barely enough room for anything else. But in between, and in front of, behind and around all of those attractions were motels, restaurants, souvenir shops, refreshment stands and all of the other businesses that relied on tourists (and vice versa) to make a vacation memorable.

One thing that all of these enterprises had in common was their eye-catching signage. Naturally, this was a necessary part of their marketing, as each one had to find a way to stand out from the cacophonous crowd. Especially at night, the flashing neon signs in a riot of colors added greatly to the character of the beach, not to mention the characters who hung out there. It seemed that every mom-and-pop motel had its own clientele that delighted in returning year after year, sometimes for decades.

Since it would be impossible to give equal time to every one of the motels that called the beach their home, in this chapter, we will be featuring only those with the most notable signage. The same rule applies to restaurants, although there were far fewer of those along the strip than there were motels. Images of souvenir shops are considerably scarcer, mainly because most of them were too small to issue commercial postcard photos, but we will visit a few of the more notable ones here as well.

If you and your family had a favorite place to stay or eat, and if we did not include it in this chapter, we apologize in advance. The Miracle Strip was a different sort of beast before the high-rise condos moved in to stay, and hopefully the images we have chosen will be a good representation of that long-gone epoch.

TOP: Well, if we're going to start off by looking at Miracle Strip motels, where better to begin than one called the Miracle Strip Motel? Thanks to visionary owner Barney Gray, it was situated smack dab in the middle of the action, across the street from the amusement park and under the watchful gaze of the observation tower.

BOTTOM: Today, Destin is so consumed with high-rises that there is no trace of its origins as a tiny fishing village. In 1993, this neon beauty still sat alongside U.S. 98, but even then it appeared as something of an anachronism. The Seaview disappeared from view not long afterward.

For quite some time, the Islander Motel was the last outpost on Okaloosa Island. Its neon letters on the tall rooftop TV antenna made it easy to spot from a distance when there was nothing else around. (Of course, this promotional photo provides other sights, too.) With its aqua color scheme, the Islander was a quintessential beach motel.

Holiday Inn ®#1
PANAMA CITY,
FLORIDA

Holiday Inn ®#2
PANAMA CITY
BEACH,
FLORIDA

U.S. HIGHWAY 98 DOWNTOWN

on St. Andrew Bay

#1 711 W. BEACH DRIVE   PH. 904 763-4622

U.S. HIGHWAY 98

on The Gulf of Mexico

#2 12907 W. HIGHWAY 98   PH. 904 234-3344

Enjoy Dining at

Judon's Restaurant Lounge

beautiful with a
view of our beach

Specializing in
Steaks & Seafood

Santa Rosa Blvd.
Okaloosa Island
243-9181

Holiday Inn
FT WALTON
BEACH, FLA

Cocktail lounge with
entertainment nightly

OWNED AND OPERATED BY DON A. MADDEN

OPPOSITE, TOP: Fort Walton Beach had a surprising number of motels that were not gulfside, on Okaloosa Island, but instead overlooked Santa Rosa Sound. Bacon's by the Sea was one of those, but just feast your peepers on that multicolored sign and the Sputnik-type Roto-Sphere at the top.

OPPOSITE, BOTTOM & ABOVE: No collection of vintage signs would be complete without Holiday Inn's blinking and flashing masterpiece known as the "Great Sign." Whether in Panama City Beach, Fort Walton Beach or elsewhere, the sight of that colorful beacon was like nirvana to travelers after a long day of driving or fun-making.

The orange roof, for many years a symbol of quality food and services, now offers the perfect fulfillment for your traveling needs. Our modern Motor Lodges are especially planned to meet every need of you and your family. We offer luxurious rooms for relaxation, a pool for a refreshing dip, a restaurant for your dining pleasure and free teletype service to assure advanced reservations . . . the ultimate in comfort and convenience . . . all at sensible prices.

HOWARD JOHNSON'S
MOTOR LODGE
4126 MOBILE HWY. AT CIRCLE   Hwy. 90 & 98
PENSACOLA, FLORIDA   GL 6-5731

After decades as America's biggest restaurant chain, Howard Johnson's finally got into the motor lodge business. The eateries had used a silhouette of Simple Simon and the Pieman as their logo; the motor lodges kept Simon but paired him with a figure evoking a popular song of the day, "The Old Lamplighter of Long, Long Ago." *Brian Rucker collection.*

Even in transition from a restaurant chain to primarily a lodging brand, Howard Johnson's retained its roadside identity with a bright orange roof topped by a teal-colored spire. This location in Fort Walton Beach made a spectacular sight at night. *Brian Rucker collection.*

As former Howard Johnson's Motor Lodges were converted into other brands, their orange roofs were usually painted over. In 2008, the Fort Walton Beach roof was beginning to emerge from its latter-day paint job, betraying its true origin to anyone savvy enough to notice.

The Best Western chain also had signage that was impossible to ignore at night, with a flashing crown that pierced the darkness. On Okaloosa Island, it was paired with the neon artwork of the Aloha Village motel—yet another example of the Miracle Strip going after a South Seas flavor.

The Ramada Inn of Fort Walton Beach had its own glowing neon but was best remembered for the waterfall in front and its collection of bars and lounges. With attendants and their toga togs such as those in Nero's Nook, the eccentric emperor might have set fire to Rome without needing any matches.

Ready to stop for a bite or two to eat? This Pensacola coffee shop was part of the popular 1930s–40s fried chicken franchise known as Chicken in the Rough, several years before Colonel Sanders began his efforts to corner the chicken market.

The Staff Restaurant in Fort Walton Beach was a local fixture beginning in 1931, but its exterior decoration and signage tended to change quite often. At the time of this mid-1960s ad, Staff was sporting the same aqua paint job so often seen on motels (such as the Islander), augmented with giant cutout sea-creature decorations. Staff closed in 2013, but the building—minus the seafood artwork—has remained to serve other purposes.

OLD SMOKEY

COMBINATION BARBECUE PLATTER

Barbecue Sandwich,
Plate or Pound to go

15928 West Highway 98 • Phone 234-5000
Panama City Beach, Florida

OPEN 6 A.M.

SPECIALTY OF THE HOUSE

GULF FRESH
SEAFOOD

$2.69 CHAR-BROILED STEAKS
T-BONE STEAK 10 oz.

INCLUDES CHOICE OF POTATO,
SALAD AND HOT ROLLS

There was perhaps nothing overly distinctive about the Old Smokey steak and barbecue house, except that its architecture and signage would have made it look more at home in Gatlinburg or Pigeon Forge than in Panama City Beach.

Popeyes Fried Chicken, of course, is still strong-arming its way through all its poultry competitors but no longer uses this early signage, as seen on Eglin Parkway in 1981. As a bonus, note the equally extinct neon Krispy Kreme sign (and a portion of the green roof) next door.

Residents and tourists alike still have fond memories of Fort Walton Beach's Seagull Restaurant. We can all be grateful that this 1979 advertisement managed to capture that amazing twilight shot of its neon sign beginning to glow.

OPPOSITE: Okay, enough eating—let's get back to the area attractions. Hopefully, the Gulfarium will always be an Okaloosa Island mainstay, but its roadside signage has seen quite an evolution. The 1950s photo dates from its aqua-and-yellow period, when it stood alone among the sand dunes. By the time of the 1993 shot, the sign featured a neon porpoise jumping through a neon hoop over and over again. The Gulfarium has been through several other sign designs since then.

ABOVE: While the Gulfarium has remained in the same building since its opening in 1955, layers of remodeling have rendered it almost unrecognizable. At the time of this 1979 photo, it still looked pretty much as it had for the previous twenty years, with its aqua-and-yellow paint job and a giant cutout Flipper on its central pylon.

ABOVE & LEFT: Some businesses decided to use concrete statuary as their identification. This small snack bar adjoining the west side of Goofy Golf had a dimensional representation of the famous Icee trademark polar bear. There is a high probability that the Icee Bear was another of Lee Koplin's creations, not only because it was on his land but also because it featured the same outstretched right hand, for photo ops, as Goofy Golf's monkey and Tombstone Territory's genie. *Jeri Good collection; Mat Raymond collection.*

OPPOSITE: Speaking of the Icee frozen drink, the Panama City Beach strip was once lined with temporary refreshment stands shaped like giant Icee cups. After they had all been slurped dry, it is believed that some of the recycled Icee cups formed the base for this similar string of ice cream stands. *John Margolies collection.*

Then there was the case of this behemoth, which was often advertised as "the largest statue in Florida" (as if there was a competition for such). It was originally Sir Loin, emblem of a Panama City Beach steakhouse of the same name, but it later received concrete surgery and emerged as King Neptune. Despite public support, the crumbling old monarch fell victim to local sign ordinances and was dethroned in 2004.

Was the Green Knight in service to King Neptune, or was he a contemporary of Sir Loin at the Round Table? Either way, he stood on the border of Destin and Fort Walton Beach to advertise his namesake restaurant and lounge. After suffering one joust too many with periodic hurricanes, he succumbed in 1998.

There is nothing quite like the glow of neon, especially when many different signs are placed in proximity. This nighttime view of Long Beach Resort would have been an incredible sight at any time, but on a summer evening in the 1950s or 1960s, it seemed more magical than Disneyland.

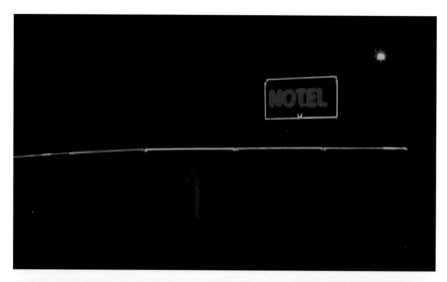

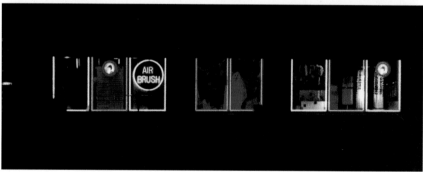

Businesses large and small employed neon to draw attention to themselves, especially when there was little else to make anyone notice their buildings at night. Both of these photos were taken in Panama City Beach in 1993; the motel's pink-and-green outline undoubtedly dated back several decades, while the airbrush shop represented the more recent reemergence of neon as an advertising tool.

OPPOSITE, TOP: Of course, souvenirs were another huge part of any vacation. From 1949 until 2002, Allan Davis Seashells in Gulf Breeze was one of the largest souvenir suppliers on the Miracle Strip, servicing not only tourists but also chain stores across the country.

OPPOSITE, BOTTOM: A very similar line of seaside souvenirs could be found at Panama City's Pink Clam. There seemed to be no end to the types of knickknacks that could be fashioned from shells of all sizes, from the giant conch shells to tiny sand dollars. Particularly common were dioramas with shells forming a backdrop of sorts for plastic flamingoes and palm trees.

Even resort cities had their downtown shopping areas, though their clientele was mostly local people instead of out-of-state tourists. Here is Panama City's Harrison Avenue in 1956, when signage and storefronts were pushing the limits of how colorful they could be. It appears Texaco had discovered the visibility potential of fluorescent ink.

By contrast, Fort Walton Beach's main drag jumped right into the souvenirs racket with a hearty will. If you had forgotten any vacation essentials before you left home, there were plenty of stores ready to replenish your supply.

As with everywhere else, downtown shopping was eventually supplanted by shopping centers, whose huge parking lots eliminated the main drawback to street-side shops. Of course, shopping centers would themselves be replaced by malls, but the popular-opinion pendulum has now swung back in the other direction, and open-air shopping centers are again the rage.

TOP: Convenience stores were there to make themselves, well, convenient. The Jr. chain of stores was seemingly everywhere throughout the Miracle Strip, each sporting this logo character who looked something like Dagwood Bumstead without the unruly hair.

BOTTOM: Even though there are entire books documenting the story of Stuckey's, we cannot neglect to mention the location that stood at the foot of Panama City's Hathaway Bridge from 1954 until being dropped from the Stuckey's chain in 1999. The building was obliterated when the highway was widened in the early 2000s. Owners Dennis and Martha Rich took pride in keeping their store almost exactly the same as it had been on opening day—a rare goal indeed in the rapidly changing retail world.

CHAPTER SIX

MELODY MAY'S MIRACLE STRIP

If the Miracle Strip, and Panama City Beach in particular, could have been said to have a face, it would have been the lovely one belonging to model Melody May. Her good looks were splashed across the media, in both glorious color and crisp black and white, and she certainly did her part to attract visitors.

In 1965, eighteen-year-old Melody responded to an ad offering the opportunity to be a model representing Panama City Beach in its marketing campaign. Melody went to the auditions along with one of her older sisters, who took one look at the competition and decided not to even try. Melody said that she felt that she was lacking in some of the more obvious physical attributes possessed by the other applicants, but she gave it her best. She was told later that she was chosen to be the Miracle Strip model primarily on the basis of her wholesome girl-next-door face, particularly her smile, and her mile-long legs that were toned from years of dancing.

As the photos in this final chapter will show, Melody was pressed into service to advertise a wide range of Panama City Beach attractions, but particularly the ones connected with the Miracle Strip Amusement Park. In later years, she laughed about the idea that most people assumed she was getting paid for her modeling work; she said the thought of asking for money never entered her mind. As far as she was concerned, she was only doing her part to attract more business to her hometown.

Although Melody is no longer with us, her image will continue to be seen wherever vintage photos and postcards from the Miracle Strip are published. She was as much a part of the area as the amusement parks, the sand and the sea oats, and we are most pleased to be able to close our retrospective with a selection of her best moments.

OPPOSITE, TOP LEFT: Photos such as this demonstrate why Melody was chosen to be the emblem of the Miracle Strip. She said that even before her modeling days, when she would walk along the beach in her bikini, total strangers would stop her and ask to take her photo. Maybe that would seem a bit creepy today, but at the time, she just considered it flattering. *Melody May collection.*

OPPOSITE, TOP RIGHT: Okay, we know you've seen it before, and in all likelihood you will see it again—many times. This was the most reproduced photo of Melody, and it isn't hard to see why. Even today it can be found on any number of "retro" souvenir items, paying tribute to the two shapely objects it features.

OPPOSITE, BOTTOM: Someone must have been thinking of the famous poster for that horror movie *The Attack of the 50 Foot Woman*. No, Melody was actually of average height, but this miniature model of the Top O' the Strip tower turns up in several different photos of the era; its current whereabouts are unknown.

ABOVE: Made during the same photo session as the famous "rearview shot" we have seen, this pose originally featured Melody balancing the miniature tower in her left hand. For usage in brochures and other publicity, the tower was replaced by the hourglass artwork. Melody's beaming smile remained untouched.

OPPOSITE & THIS PAGE, TOP: Contrary to what one might think, not all of Melody's photo work involved her bikini. For a series of Miracle Strip Amusement Park postcards, she adopted a more big-sisterly look. Yes, MSAP added one more miniature train ride to the others that were tootling around the beach attractions.

THIS PAGE, BOTTOM: Part of Melody's charm, both on and off camera, is that she never took herself too seriously and was certainly not impressed by her own image. When Val Valentine's Old House was built at MSAP, Melody covered her white swimsuit with a shroud and allowed her face to be painted ghostly white, even though the actual attraction employed no live actors.

OPPOSITE: For Jungle Land, Melody's characterizations seemed to more closely evoke Raquel Welch in *One Million Years B.C.* than the South Seas setting. She greatly enjoyed the many different poses and settings the photographers crafted for her, and she was game for whatever crazy idea they concocted next.

ABOVE: After the previous photo, standing on the slippery artificial rocks, Melody found that her feet were covered with the tar that was used to make them waterproof. Val Valentine captured this classic shot of his son helping out and getting an up-close view of Melody's long stems, thus becoming (however briefly) the luckiest guy on the beach.

OPPOSITE: Again proving Melody's willingness to do just about anything for a photo, these Jungle Land images show her ability to ham it up with assorted props. Her facial expressions did much to add to the poses cooked up by the photographers. *Florida State Archives collection.*

ABOVE: So, just how many spring breakers do you suppose this image brought into Jungle Land? We'd have to assume they probably multiplied like rabbits, wouldn't you say?

Although Panama City Beach's tourist season traditionally followed a strict Memorial Day to–Labor Day schedule, the publicity machine never stopped grinding out material. For this Christmas shot, Melody dressed like Santa's helper and used the sugar-white sand as a substitute for snow. *Melody May collection.*

OPPOSITE, TOP: In the spring of 2013, Melody returned to the former Jungle Land (aka Alvin's Magic Mountain Mall) to re-create some of her long-ago poses. Tragically, she passed away at age sixty-seven in February 2015 after a brief battle with pancreatic cancer.

OPPOSITE, BOTTOM: But let's not end on a sad note. This is the way we all want to remember Melody May. Everything is perfect: her expression, her pose, her outfit and, most of all, that slogan that sums up the now-long-gone Miracle Strip in one three-letter word: FUN. *Kenneth Redd collection.*

BIBLIOGRAPHY

Flynn, Stephen J. *Florida: Land of Fortune*. New York: Van Rees Press, 1962.

Genovese, Peter. *Roadside Florida: The Definitive Guide to the Kingdom of Kitsch*. Mechanicsburg, PA: Stackpole Books, 2006.

Hollis, Tim. *Dixie before Disney: 100 Years of Roadside Fun*. Jackson: University Press of Mississippi, 1999.

———. *Florida's Miracle Strip: From Redneck Riviera to Emerald Coast*. Jackson: University Press of Mississippi, 2004.

———. *The Minibook of Minigolf*. Gainesville, FL: Seaside Publishing, 2015.

Margolies, John. *Miniature Golf*. New York: Abbeville Press, 1987.

Mormino, Gary R. *Land of Sunshine, State of Dreams: A Social History of Modern Florida*. Gainesville: University Press of Florida, 2005.

Redd, Kenneth. *Odyssey of the Enchanter: The Life and Art of Vincent E. Valentine Jr.* Canton, GA: Yawn Publishing, 2020.

Reynolds, Robert. *Simply Seagrove: An Intimate History of One of Florida's Most Beautiful Beaches.* Tucson, AZ: Emerald Waters Press, 2018.

Rucker, Brian R. *Treasures of the Panhandle: A Journey through West Florida*. Gainesville: University Press of Florida, 2011.

Smith, Jan. *Panama City Beach*. Charleston, SC: Arcadia Publishing, 2004.

Van Steenwyk, Elizabeth. *Let's Go to the Beach: A History of Sun and Fun by the Sea*. New York: Henry Holt, 2001.

ABOUT THE AUTHOR

Tim Hollis has written thirty-five books on pop culture history, a number of them concerning southeastern tourism. He also operates his own museum of vintage toys, souvenirs and other pop-culture artifacts near Birmingham, Alabama.